Edward Vine's
DORSET

TEXT BY
BARRY MILES

HALSGROVE
IN ASSOCIATION WITH
THE PETER HEDLEY GALLERY, WAREHAM

First published in 2002 by Halsgrove
Images © 2002 Edward Vine
Text © 2002 Barry Miles

British Library Cataloguing-in-Publication Data
A CIP record for this title is available from the British Library

ISBN 1 84114 199 2

HALSGROVE
Halsgrove House
Lower Moor Way
Tiverton, Devon EX16 6SS
T: 01884 243242
F: 01884 243325
www.halsgrove.com

Printed in Hong Kong by Regal Printing Ltd

Contents

EDWARD VINE

*I am grateful to the collectors of my work, who have made it possible for me to make a career out of a lifelong pleasure.
Thanks also to Profolab of Weymouth for producing excellent photographs of the paintings.*

This book is dedicated to Geraldine.

BARRY MILES

*Peter Hedley's initial introduction led to the book's concept; Steven Pugsley of Halsgrove showed continued
commitment and belief; Geraldine Vine helped me organise the text and choose the paintings; Andrew and Marilyn Leah's
contribution was very welcome. My thanks to them all for bringing this project to such a successful conclusion.*

~ *Foreword* ~

BY PETER HEDLEY

*Peter Hedley has been promoting contemporary painters and sculptors for more than
thirty years. Over half of those have been spent at the Peter Hedley Gallery in Wareham,
Dorset, where he and his wife Jennifer are very much part of the local community.*

I remember clearly my first meeting with Edward and his wife, Geraldine. They had made an appointment to show me a few of his paintings and tentatively asked my opinion. I took two of them into my stock, putting one in the window. They sold within the week.

More than fifteen years have passed since then. The sale of that painting of Shilvinghampton, near Portesham, was the first of many milestones in our near-perfect working relationship, built on mutual respect and an understanding of the vagaries of the art world.

In that world, overnight success is rare. This artist's achievements have been gained gradually by sheer hard work and application, complementing his natural talent. Geraldine has played no small part. They are a team.

Edward has a disciplined, conscientious approach to exhibitions and commissions, coupled with an emotional attachment to both subject and method. These qualities shine from his work, clearly visible to the discerning collector.

I have seen, at first hand, many of the paintings reproduced in this book and I am delighted to be asked to participate in this exciting project. Lovers of fine art and the county of Dorset will find much here in which to delight.

June 2002

SOUTHWELL

Edward

⨍ Introduction to the Artist ⨍

Dorset is the jewel in the crown of the South of England. It has beauty in all seasons, in its rolling downs, atmospheric heaths, dense woodland, gentle river valleys and highly-prized coastline. It has enough variety for any artist to be content and to spend a lifetime travelling no more than a few miles in any direction.

Edward Vine is a true Dorsetman. From the challenge of the ever-changing sea and the dramatic Heritage coast to the soft nuances of a single hedgerow daisy, the home county of this Dorset artist is his prime subject and inspiration. The constant goal is to capture natural beauty, light and atmosphere, all of which are offered in abundance on his doorstep.

His paintings are enjoyed in private and corporate collections world-wide.

EARLY YEARS

Edward was born during an air raid in 1943, under his aunt's kitchen table in New Street, Weymouth, only yards from the sea. He remained in the neighbouring family home, a Grade II listed Georgian cottage, until the mid-1980s, when he moved to his present Portland location.

His grandfather, Joe Vine, was Cox of Weymouth Lifeboat from 1931 to 1945 and had served in the days when brave men manned oars to rescue lives. Joe was a well-known character around the harbour, as was his son, Ted, a carpenter for the Local Authority, working mainly on harbour maintenance. Edward remembers his father going off to diver training in the tanks at Portsmouth, no mean feat for a non-swimmer. The leaded boots and massive helmets of the old diving suits were extremely uncomfortable, but made possible the essential work on the harbour walls.

The extended family was very close – sisters, cousins, aunts and uncles – Edward's childhood memories are very happy. Many hours were spent around the harbour or out in Weymouth Bay in the family boat *Meg*. He and his father would row across the Bay to Ringstead or out along the Portland Breakwater to fish. Neither could swim and not a life jacket in sight. How times have changed…!

PULPIT ROCK - EV

The influences of these contented days have remained. The love of the sea was clearly instilled by his father's side of the family. An early interest in drawing and painting was particularly encouraged by his mother's two brothers, Bob and Arthur Ozzard, both being lifelong amateur artists. No surprise then that the boy's interests should merge and he should be found often on the harbourside with pencil and paper.

Apprenticed at the age of fifteen to a local horologist and jeweller, he stayed with the firm for twenty-six years, until it was sold on the owner's retirement. Working on everything from the cheapest wrist-watch to antique long-case clocks, from hand-made jewellery to the most valuable antique diamonds – the years slipped away. The detailed, intricate benchwork required dexterity, concentration, and dedication – all qualities more than useful for an artist.

ARTISTIC DEVELOPMENT

Through those years, his pencils and brushes were rarely still – solely for his own enjoyment and self-instruction. In his early twenties, he rented for several years a 'studio' – an upstairs room in a condemned building behind a butcher's shop. It had electric light, a paraffin stove and a few mice for company. Art became a subject to be taken more seriously. It was in this room that his own talents were nurtured and his admiration for those of the Old Masters put to good use. He spent hours making pencil copies of drawings by Michaelangelo and oil copies of works by Rubens. Still life items – flowers, old boots, bottles etc. – were set up on the table and the midnight oil burnt regularly.

Edward also spent time on abstract works, oil canvases inspired by the shapes of the natural world and by a strong feeling that human emotion and the senses could be depicted in graphic form.

In the late '70s, these abstracts were quite suddenly left behind in the pursuit of one goal, which has dominated Edward's artistic life since. He realised that he had never seriously attempted to master landscape painting. As for many budding artists, the genius of John Constable had been a shining light, but the prospect of working 'en plein air' had been too daunting. The following years saw him take up that challenge and, indeed, he considers the journey he commenced at that time to be never-ending.

Many Sundays, in all seasons were spent in the countryside around Dorchester with pencil and pad. He remembers sitting for hours drawing, wearing half-mittens, in the relative comfort of his warm car, occasionally running the engine to defrost the windscreen – a luxury after so many previous outings on his old Lambretta. Thorncombe Woods, Came Down and Woodsford were particular favourites for these trips.

It is regrettable that so few of the products of these early efforts have survived. Edward saw them as a means to an end, each sketch only providing him with the required practice, a stepping stone to the next one. His early paintings were viewed in much the same way, not as finished works to be framed, but as part of the learning curve.

A NEW START

On his employer's retirement in the early 1980s, Edward's life changed significantly. He had been courting Geraldine in the mid-1960s. After a break of twenty years in their relationship, she decided to accept his proposal. He now had a wife, a new home and was self-employed in his two crafts for the first time – he had started to sell the occasional painting.

Local art and craft shows provided the initial spur to early sales, together with small commissions in pencil, line and wash, pen and ink, watercolour and acrylic. The subject matter was varied, interesting and sometimes hungry! One sitter, a border collie called Tess, ate more digestive biscuits than could have been paid for by the price of the finished work. A more unusual request was for a watercolour of 'a certain size', which could be stowed safely aboard a US Naval submarine on its voyage to its captain's home in the States. Painting was usually undertaken in 'tired time' – after a full day at the watchmaking bench. One or two Dorset galleries sold Edward's work and spring 1991 brought his first one-man exhibition at the library in Weymouth. This was followed by other shows in Dorchester, at Laura Wood Homer's gallery.

Gradually, the numbers of commissions and the demand for his paintings increased. More and more time was spent at the easel and eventually, the watchmaker's eyeglass was set aside permanently, with no reluctance on Edward's part. He was now painting nearly every day and supplying a number of galleries.

PETER HEDLEY AND THE PURBECK HILLS

The link with the Peter Hedley Gallery in Wareham was forged in 1988, with Edward's first one-man show there in 1994. Edward has exhibited at other galleries in Dorset but the working relationship with Peter has always been special. Their fifth, biennial exhibition took place in spring 2002 and many of the paintings reproduced in this book are from that exhibition.

Around eighty new works are unveiled at each show and the Dorset landscape exclusively provides the subject matter. In latter years, Poole Harbour, the Purbeck Hills and the Studland coastline have featured heavily. No matter how many visits are made to this stunning area, each time it is seen afresh. Autumn here is his favourite season. Amongst his favourite commissions have been those for the Royal Society for the Protection of Birds of their reserves around Poole Harbour.

Edward exhibited three paintings with the Royal Society of Marine Artists at the Mall Galleries in London in 2001. They all depicted land at Studland owned by the National Trust, part of the Purbeck Heritage Coast project. The project has been awarded the Council of Europe Diploma for its outstanding environment, where visitors are welcome to enjoy the wildlife, landscape and traditional delights of the seaside.

'MAX GATE', DORCHESTER

'Max Gate' is the Dorchester home of poet and novelist Thomas Hardy, which he designed and his brother Henry built. Hardy lived there from 1885 until his death in 1928. It was bequeathed to the National Trust in 1940 by Hardy's sister Kate, and Andrew and Marilyn Leah are the National Trust's tenants. The house and garden are open from Easter to autumn and Edward's work adds to the Dorset atmosphere of the public rooms. He feels very privileged to be the permanent Artist-in-Residence under the Leah's stewardship of the house.

WAREHAM   EV

⁓ *Influences and Working Notes* ⁓

Like most artists, Edward is inspired not only by the works of the past Masters, but also by other living artists and has a shelf of books by and about favourites. He returns consistently to those by Philip Jamison, a Dolphin member of the American Watercolour Society. He also considers Norman Battershill's paintings to have influenced him greatly, both on the printed page and on the wall. Visits to the exhibitions of individual artists or groups, such as the Royal Societies, can be interesting and stimulating.

EQUIPMENT

The fisherman with the largest range of expensive equipment doesn't always catch the biggest fish – a similar rule applies to art. Edward keeps to a very basic range of tools.

He has a wooden and an aluminium easel, both lightweight, and a modern draughtsman's board. His backless, canvas, sketching stool doubles as a useful aid for clearing overgrown footpaths. A nylon-canvas satchel carries the items for field trips, including a cyclist's water bottle and a small portable box with folding palette and water-colour pans.

Although he has acquired a selection of brushes, he has narrowed his regulars to a few. Sable and synthetic are used for watercolours; hog and synthetic are the choice for acrylic and oil. Similarly, the tempting array of paint on display at art suppliers poses little problem. Tubes are preferred to pans in the studio and he uses exclusively non-fugitive tints of the best artist quality, for permanence.

Although Bockingford and Whatman papers of various weights are hand-stretched in the studio, Edward often uses watercolour board. For acrylics, he likes acrylic-gesso primed art board or a medium-weight, fine grain **not** paper. A family member on holiday happened upon a bankrupt paper mill in Scotland some years ago and this resulted in Edward cutting and binding a large supply of his own

sketchbooks. He uses 2B, 4B and 6B pencils, but occasionally works with charcoal.

An elderly Ricoh camera, with print film, is in permanent use. Edward agrees with Pietro Annigoni's view of the camera in art:

> *A hasty sketch set down under the impulse of a spontaneous emotion of my own is for me a thousand times more vital and evocative.*

However, the camera has its place as a reference tool, as long as nature is the prime source of both inspiration and information. Work is never copied or undertaken solely from photographs and the common practice of projecting images on to a surface is never employed.

Binoculars are useful for checking the shapes of distant objects and Ordnance Survey maps for identifying them – and for finding his way back to the car! Most importantly, on field trips, he carries a

FERRYBRIDGE — EV

flask of coffee and sandwiches. More are kept in the car awaiting his return, as experience has proved that the days are almost always longer than planned!

FIELD TRIPS

Earlier in his career, many hours were spent painting outdoors, but Edward now undertakes many complete paintings in the studio. Frequent sketching trips are an enjoyable essential and a love of the local flora and fauna adds to this enjoyment. An advantage of sitting quietly is that wildlife may pause nearby. The shy Dartford Warbler and Sika deer have both been encountered recently in this manner. Geraldine always accompanies Edward, usually taking photographs and birdwatching while he works.

Pencil or watercolour sketches are made on site and the atmosphere of the subject landscape absorbed at length, with mental and physical notes made on colour. Half-closing the eyes to view the landscape can eliminate detail, leading to an appreciation of simplified tones and values. These sketches vary enormously: some are broadly handled and others more detailed. Hopefully, the sketch will highlight and reflect a freshness and spontaneity that can be revisited later in the studio. The time lapse between sketching and painting can be very short and that midnight oil is still frequently burnt!

CHOICE OF MEDIA

Occasionally, a commission is requested in a particular medium. More often it is suggested initially by the subject matter. Sometimes, this leads to a second, completely different handling of the same subject in another medium. Sand dunes, for example, respond well to both watercolour and acrylic, each imparting its own special quality. Edward likes to switch medium frequently, to keep the approach fresh, but rarely has more than one work in progress at a time.

WATERCOLOURS, ACRYLICS AND GOUACHE

Standing to paint, Edward constantly walks back and forth to vary the view, sitting several yards from the easel for periods of contemplation and planning. A mount is used at varying stages to 'hold in' the composition and give an early guide to the finished painting.

The aluminium easel, which tilts to give a completely flat surface, or the draughtsman's board for larger works, are both ideal for watercolours. Some watercolours require meticulous planning and some evolve with a mind of their own. Often, even an experienced artist doesn't know into which category a project will fall until he has commenced. This elusive quality is part of the medium's appeal to both artist and collector alike.

Gouache is an opaque watercolour, soluble even when it has dried on the paper. Several gouaches usually feature in Edward's one-man exhibitions.

Acrylic is another opaque water-medium. It differs from gouache in that it dries very quickly and is insoluble when dry, so cannot be lifted from the surface. It can be used direct from the tube or diluted to various strengths with water or acrylic 'medium'. This versatility and expressiveness make it his favourite. He feels it gives him full freedom to change direction as and when required, at any point in the painting process. Mixing all three water-media together can give exciting results.

COLOURS

Harmony can be achieved by using very few colours. Edward often uses no more than four or five tints in acrylics and watercolours. The basic palette choice for each medium varies slightly:

SANDSFOOT   EV

ACRYLIC

Cadmium Red
Ultramarine
Cobalt Blue
Cerulean
Cadmium Yellow
Burnt Sienna
Yellow Ochre

WATERCOLOUR

Quinacridone Red
Ultramarine
Cobalt Blue
Prussian Blue
Raw Sienna
Burnt Sienna
Viridian

Other colours are substituted and added as required – for example acrylic Quinacridone Red could be used on skies or flowers.

OTHER MEDIA

Edward used to paint solely in oils, but recently has done only a few each year, largely because of his love of acrylics. It is on his 'one day I will…' list to spend a year working mainly on oils, when time allows.

Pastels have been a particular pleasure, because of their direct contact to nature and the beauty of their finish. However, to his dismay, he now finds the dust irritates his eyes, resulting in a reduction in the number of pastels he produces. Oil pastels would be a potential second choice and more work with these is also on the above-mentioned wish-list. Artists never stop learning and experimenting.

PRESENTATION

Final presentation is highly important and Edward enjoys taking responsibility for this. The process of painting can be physically and emotionally draining and framing can make a relaxing change on a difficult day. His framer supplies the constructed frames and glass, but Edward hand-cuts the double mounts and assembles the finished work. He uses a mapping pen and brushes to paint the delicate watercolour washlines that decorate some of the mounts.

❧ *The Paintings* ❧

The paintings that follow are a representative selection of Edward's work from recent years, separated into six groups. Four of these are the areas of Dorset on which he has concentrated during this period: Poole Harbour, The Isle of Purbeck, Studland and Old Harry, and his home-turf of Weymouth and Portland.

The group entitled 'Quiet Corners' includes paintings from around Dorset, bound by the common theme of peace and beauty.

Edward has commented on each subject in these five groups, with a personal note on the location and its attraction for him as an artist.

The last section, 'Max Gate', depicts, almost by default, the landscapes of Thomas Hardy, with a short quotation from one of his works. The paintings were not undertaken expressly with Hardy in mind, but much of Dorset is inextricably linked with his genius. Edward's subject matter in paint is often that of Hardy's in prose or poetry.

Rockley - EV

⇜ *Poole Harbour* ⇝

Poole Harbour is one of the world's largest natural harbours, with a sixty-mile shoreline and a fascinating maritime history, dating from the pre-Romans. Although container shipping departs daily and the harbour has an active fishing fleet, it is best known for its ferry trade to the Continent and its leisure and tourism industry.

The commercial drilling of oil commenced in the late 1970s, threatening the harbour's environment and atmosphere. The development appears to have been achieved by BP sympathetically and with minimum impact, winning the Queen's Award for Environmental Achievement in 1995. Adjacent to the oilfields is the Reserve at Arne, a major success story for the Royal Society for the Protection of Birds. There are seven other nature reserves, national and local, including one run by the Dorset Wildlife Trust on Brownsea. The island is the largest of several in the harbour and is now owned by the National Trust.

Sandbanks boasts some of the globe's most expensive real estate, but the area's sun, sea and sand can be enjoyed freely. From here, the chain-link ferry crosses to the Studland spit. Little sandy beaches, inlets and outcrops stud the harbour's south and south-eastern shores, each with a special character. These are at the top of a list of Edward's favourite places, both to work and for quiet meditation.

Edward has been able to have access to both private and RSPB land not open to the public, in order to complete commissions. These visits have served to extend his admiration for and attraction to the Harbour's shores.

From Smedmore Hill
acrylic (19 x 24in)

'The more adventurous hang-glide from here down over Kimmeridge Bay, but I'm inclined to sit to enjoy the views – looking north-east sets Corfe Castle and the harbour beyond into context.'

19

Sandbanks
acrylic (10 x 11in)

'Poole Harbour has ten active boatyards; this one forms an almost incidental backdrop to the real attraction for me – the horizontals and verticals reflected at low tide.'

To Poole from Sandbanks
acrylic (10 x 20in)

'Windsurfers set off from this corner beneath Evening Hill, providing me with excellent practice at capturing movement quickly in pencil.'

Harbourside Coffee Break
acrylic (8 x 10in)

'Fresh off the *Bramblebush Bay* ferry from Sandbanks, I find a pause to drink in the view of the harbour and its islands is most welcome.'

Evening Sails, Brownsea
acrylic (13 x 18in)

'Evening sun lights up the distant Purbeck Hills. If you listen closely with your imagination, the faint strains of Mozart from the Open Air Opera on Brownsea waft across the water.'

Low Water, Poole Harbour
acrylic (14 x 12in)

'This subject poses three challenges: clouds, their reflections and how not to sink too far into the muddy sand on my stool. I always carry a copy of the tide tables, to make maximum use of time and, of course, for safety.'

Poole Harbour, Studland
acrylic   (7 x 14in)

'This particular boathouse always fills me with romantic notions of leaving modern life behind. The feeling wears off when I arrive home and turn on the central heating before enjoying a hot shower!'

Bramblebush Bay
watercolour (19 x 24in)

'I don't know who was responsible for naming these idyllic corners, but they certainly added to their charm. The distant island is Furzey, from Furze, the local name for gorse.'

Rounding Harry Point, Brownsea
acrylic (14 x 12in)

'Shingle, possibly distributed for conservation purposes at various sites around the harbour's southern shores, makes an attractive addition to the sand.'

Harbour Heath
acrylic (19 x 24in)

'The protected heathland adjacent to the Studland Ferry Road is a year-round gift for any artist. I particularly love the ochre and browns in sunlight when the heather is not blooming.'

Redhorn Lake
acrylic (19 x 24in)

'Silver birches dance like ballerinas and the little egret is a regular visitor to feed, making this a very special place.'

Harbour Moon
acrylic (13 x 15in)

'I had the idea for this painting after a downpour when sunlight turned this narrow path into a shining stream. I just converted the values to those of moonlight.'

White Sails, Poole
acrylic (7 x 14in)

'The red cliff on the shores of Redhorn Lake makes a colourful reflection in the water. More of this sandstone is found on the Brownsea coast, at nearby Red End Point, and, more famously, on the Isle of Wight.'

Come the Evening
acrylic (10 x 20in)

'Redhorn Quay at dusk, with the Goathorn spit beyond. An on-site, water-colour sketch of the sky complemented an earlier pencil drawing. The day turned out to be longer than planned.'

Redhorn
acrylic (17 x 23in)

'With its backdrop of islands, Redhorn Quay glows all year round. It's common to see yachts moored overnight and fishermen snoozing on the beach between catches.'

Evening, Poole Harbour
acrylic (19 x 24in)

'Brand's Bay, in the shadow of the Purbeck Hills, is at the south-eastern corner of the harbour and, in my view, is one of the most beautiful stretches of water in the county.'

Mead Point
acrylic (19 x 24in)

'This southern end of Brand's Bay drains almost completely at low tide, leaving only rivulets amongst the seagrasses; Ower Passage and Goathorn can be seen in the distance.'

Across Newton Bay
acrylic (17 x 23in)

'Public footpaths give access to much of the harbour's shoreline, including these fields overlooking Cleavel Point. The usual group of inquisitive cows joined us on this visit.'

Still Waters
acrylic (10 x 20in)

'Brand's Bay at its best – one of those subjects when less can definitely be more.'

Cleavel
acrylic (13 x 15in)

'Cleavel Point forms the western entrance to the mouth of horse-shoe-shaped Newton Bay. There is access nearby on public foot-paths, but the point itself is private land.'

Game Copse, Poole Harbour
acrylic (13 x 24in)

'The shores of Newton Bay in glorious sunshine – the afternoon went so quickly, we had to make our way back to the car with the aid of a torch.'

West from Cleavel Point
acrylic (13 x 18in)

'This is close to the famous Ower Quay, Purbeck's chief port until the eigh-
teenth century, when Swanage took over the shipping of stone. It is difficult
now to see Ower as a hive of commercial activity.'

Clouds over Arne
acrylic (8 x 10in)

'Across the water to Froxen Copse at the RSPB's reserve at Arne, on one of the best days for cloud studies – sunshine and showers.'

Bramble and Reed
watercolour   (16 x 10in)

'I started to sketch for a full landscape, but was drawn instead to the windblown uprights of sienna against the pale azure sky. Sometimes just a shape or colour can be enough to prompt a painting.'

42

Rockley Sands
acrylic (10 x 20in)

'Rockley has a large caravan site, but it is easy to ignore when the scenery is so magnificent. The Romans chose well when they established Poole's first port at nearby Hamworthy.'

☙ *Isle of Purbeck* ❧

Misnamed the 'Isle' of Purbeck, this beautiful area's western boundary is roughly drawn by a line from Wareham to the sea and its northern boundary is Poole Harbour. Its history is one of its stone. The Romans commenced the commercial quarrying of the Purbeck-Portland limestone which, with the higher-quality, harder limestone called Purbeck Marble, still forms part of the local economy. It is in evidence in every local community, but nowhere more so than at Corfe, where the eleventh-century castle stands on a knoll in a break in the Purbeck Ridgeway, the spine of the Isle. This runs west to east, falling dramatically to the sea at the end of Ballard Down, above Swanage.

The last miles of the South West Coastal Path run along this coastline and its numerous delights are well known. The steep path from Hambury Tout to the car park at Lulworth Cove is walked by a quarter of a million people each year. Yet, go at the right time of day or year, to the right spot and you could think the land and seascapes have been spread out just for your personal pleasure. Edward is still finding new material throughout the Isle, but never tires of revisiting previous haunts. Each varying angle, light and weather condition produces differing results.

One certain place of annual pilgrimage is Worth Matravers, for a crab-salad tea after a day's work at Seacombe or Winspit – a tradition begun on his honeymoon.

Along the Purbeck Ridge
acrylic (11 x 15in)

'From the summit of Creech Barrow, the ridge of the Purbeck Hills runs east to the sea, dominating the landscape. Although it looks inviting, we've never walked it in its entirety, always getting side-tracked.'

45

The Devil's Horse Ride
watercolour (5 x 11in)

'The path from Ballard Down to Handfast Point is also known as Old Nick's Ground. I suspect this may be the older name of the two. The paper has been allowed to show alongside the watercolour paint, heightening the whiteness of the cliffs and stacks.'

Pier, Swanage
watercolour (7 x 14in)

'The locals of Swanage can be justly proud of their achievement in restoring their pier to its former glory. It was closely inspected on a family day-trip to the seaside and caused a great deal of excitement and admiration.'

Above Durdle
watercolour (14 x 12in)

'If you like a steep climb on your walk, this is the place to come. We approached from above the lovingly-named Scratchy Bottom, via the summit of Bat's Head and then down to Durdle, with lots of pauses en-route – for sketching, of course!'

48

Peveril Point
gouache (13 x 18in)

'The hidden under-water ledges at Peveril, Swanage, were a notorious hazard long ago for ships – easy to imagine, even now on a calm evening.'

Fossil Forest, Lulworth
acrylic (18 x 14in)

'Not many of my subjects are nearly 200 million years old; these fossilized tree stumps are well sign-posted and worth the climb east from Lulworth Cove, up on to the Bindon Range.'

50

Autumn Coastline
acrylic (13 x 18in)

'I try to remember to check the local paper before visiting the Purbeck Hills, to see if the Army Range Walks are open to the public, so avoiding any disappointment. This particular walk takes you west from Kimmeridge.'

Down to the Cove
acrylic (13 x 18in)

'Even at peak times, the crowds at Lulworth can be avoided, if a longer walk and a bit of hillside climbing on steeper footpaths are no problem. Besides, the beauty of the Cove is best appreciated from above.'

Above Stair Hole, Lulworth
acrylic (18 x 14in)

'I didn't know that the distinctive shaping of the layers of twisted rock strata at Stair Hole is known as "The Lulworth Crumple" until someone told me while I was sketching here. My choice was the trees and the shadows on the grassy paths, but the Crumple just features on the left.'

Dorset Village
gouache (7 x 16in)

'Corfe, approached from Church Knowle, by the footpath immediately beneath Knowle Hill. It is an unusual view, because the eye can cut out the castle altogether at this angle, giving the village top-billing for a change.'

Corfe Castle
acrylic (13 x 15in)

'The softness of the foliage contrasts starkly with the historic ruins, seen from my favourite vantage point of Norden. Although it is arguably a hackneyed subject, I immensely enjoy painting the castle, so I keep doing so.'

Boathuts, Kimmeridge
acrylic (10 x 20in)

'Internationally famous as a unique site for divers, this bay has kept its peaceful atmosphere intact. Even the nodding-donkey oil drill, present since the 1960s, has not overly disturbed the calm. The bay's awkward access could be responsible for this – long may it remain so.'

Plantation Pines, Creech
acrylic (17 x 23in)

'We stumbled on these majestic trees while on foot to East Holme from Creech. I went back the next day to give them my full attention.'

Path to Worth
acrylic (10 x 20in)

'As an alternative to the Priest's Way from Worth Matravers, we sometimes take this path to Winspit, which winds down through honeysuckle and parsley to the sea.'

Dorset Coastline
acrylic (14 x 12in)

'Swyre Head and Bat's Head, with the Durdle beach, really do need these figures included to emphasise their grand scale.'

59

On to Daggers Gate
acrylic (10 x 20in)

'It was very windy and we had tucked ourselves into the hedge for lunch, after which I sketched Portland, off to the west. Two walkers stopped to chat, as walkers often do, passing on their way from Ringstead Bay to Lulworth – an enjoyable half-hour spent in good company.'

60

Edward Vine

Hartland Foxgloves
acrylic (23 x 17in)

'We found these in a magical corner of Hartland Moor, while I was working on a commission. I returned later in the week to make the sketches for this painting and disturbed a Sika deer browsing just a yard from the flowers.'

To Middlebere Farm
watercolour (7 x 15in)

'The farm, run by the National Trust, overlooks Hartland Moor, home of all six species of British reptile. I've not come across any of those, but I have seen the wild ponies, which play a part in the management of the heathland. A hide, converted from an old railway carriage, is provided for birdwatchers. They may spot a Dartford Warbler if they are lucky.'

Edge of Hartland Moor
acrylic (14 x 12in)

'My sketch books are full of tree studies, but they don't all feature in finished paintings. These have made it to the easel.'

63

Four Fields, Wareham
acrylic (8 x 10in)

'Peter Hedley told me about this gem of a path at Wareham, leading down to Swineham Point on Poole Harbour. I can imagine it being used by smugglers with their kegs of rum in days long gone!'

After the Rain
acrylic   (8 x 10in)

'Swineham Point, at Wareham, looks across to Arne Hill on the far side of the Wareham Channel. Low-lying and tidal, it usually provides interesting puddles for me after rain.'

By the Frome, Wareham
acrylic (13 x 15in)

'I went to the river to sketch the bridge, but the light was so brilliant over Stoborough and the water-meadows that I concentrated on that instead.'

Lady St Mary
acrylic (8 x 10in)

'It is the juxtaposition of the uprights here that make the composition work for me – the yacht masts, the church tower, the spindly tree trunks, all softened by windblown grasses and reeds.'

67

STUDLAND - EV

⤜ Studland and Old Harry ⤛

Across the Sandbank's ferry to South Haven Point, the ambience changes and bustle is soon left behind. At the height of the season, this part of the beach can be busy, but a short walk along Shell Bay provides the solution. Three-and-a-half kilometres of soft, pale sand lie between South Haven and just beyond Red End Point, near the village of Studland itself.

The National Trust, English Nature and the Dorset Trust for Nature Conservation all take part in managing land here. This is the home of the smooth snake and the sand lizard. In recent years, there has been more rapid deterioration of the dunes. Environmental damage is easily visible along the whole of the Dorset coast. With no prior intention, Edward, for some years, has been recording a changing landscape.

Erosion is nowhere clearer than at Old Harry Rocks, where Old Harry's Wife shrinks every year. Guarding Studland Bay's southern entrance, these dramatic limestone cliffs and stacks are at the eastern point of Dorset's Heritage coastline. They collectively boast some wonderful names – Old Nick's Ground (or the Devil's Horse Ride), St Lucas Leap, Handfast Point – their history jumps off the map in the written words.

At Studland Bay
acrylic (13 x 18in)

'Late-afternoon light shines on rock and sand on an autumn day at Studland. The remains of Old Harry's Wife can be seen clearly from this end of Knoll Beach, but Old Harry himself is hiding.'

69

Coming Home
acrylic (13 x 18in)

'I don't sail – my sea legs are now wobbly to say the least – but I do get jealous of those who do. These lucky people, approaching the harbour mouth at South Haven Point, had doubtless enjoyed themselves.'

Curves and Reflections
watercolour (10 x 20in)

'The beach at South Haven Point can flood most attractively from the Central Cut that drains the Little Sea. Visitors who wish to reach the shoreline must tackle the obstacle course and risk getting their feet wet.'

Distant Island
acrylic (17 x 23in)

'The islands can form useful compositional backdrops for the harbour, but can also be seen from parts of the beach. Here, Brownsea is glimpsed from the seaward side of the South Haven Peninsula, with the Ferry Road conveniently hidden behind the dunes.'

Shell Bay
acrylic (10 x 20in)

'I know the Seychelles have a warmer climate, but it's a long way to go when all this is on our doorstep – and ours has an equally exotic name! Apparently, there are far less shells on this beach in recent years.'

Low Cloud, Studland
watercolour (13 x 15in)

'This part of the beach is particularly interesting, with excellent composition available looking either south or north, as here along Shell Bay. I paint increasingly in acrylic, but this works equally for me in watercolour.'

Sand Shadows
acrylic (13 x 18in)

'Much of my childhood was spent on Weymouth Beach and I still love the feel of hot sand between my toes. Perhaps that's one reason why I get such pleasure from the Studland subjects, never tiring of them.'

Summer Skies
acrylic (17 x 23in)

'A new painting, or the inspiration for one, waits at almost every turn. Even so, the brush can move a clump of grasses from left to right, or vice-versa, to suit. It can also turn two yachts into three and change their sail colours – all part of the fun.'

Studland Breeze
acrylic (17 x 23in)

'Behind the promontory at the southern tip of Shell Bay, young marram grasses struggle to keep a firm hold. Without them, the whole eco-system of the dunes breaks down.'

Shadows, Studland
acrylic (13 x 24in)

'Shadows are rarely grey. Reds and blues used in the clouds are repeated to warm up the cool tones of the sandy slopes.'

The Walk to the Ferry
acrylic (19 x 24in)

'Half-mittens and hot drinks were called for on this bitterly cold, but brightly lit, October day. A few sprigs of lucky heather were still in flower.'

Knoll Beach
acrylic (13 x 18in)

'The red wellies were long gone before the sketch was finished, but they were the only colour note I made and form the focal point of the painting.'

80

Dunes, Studland
acrylic (13 x 15in)

'This image says it all about the area for me – the wheeling gulls have just crept into the top corner, reminding me that the sea, although not visible, is just over the horizon.'

81

Along the Tideline
acrylic (10 x 20in)

'Dried seaweed contributes a balancing of autumnal colour and defines the tideline in this study of Knoll Beach, aiding the impression of recession which I was trying to achieve.'

Waiting for the Weekend
gouache (9 x 11in)

'The National Trust dinghy park at Knoll Beach is a hive of activity on a summer weekend, but often quiet midweek, especially early and late in the season.'

Middle Beach, Studland
acrylic (17 x 23in)

'The dark shadow across the rocks and sand makes this painting work for me. Middle Beach starts at Redend Point, where coloured sandstones, similar to those on the Isle of Wight, can be seen on the rockface.'

Late in the Season
acrylic (13 x 18in)

'This area of Knoll Beach has been successfully protected by fencing to encourage the underground rooting of the marram grasses, stabilising the dunes. The posts provided me with a perfect lead-in for the eye.'

St Lucas Leap, Studland
acrylic   (11 x 15in)

'I really must get round to finding out who St Lucas was and why he had to leap! Meanwhile, it's a subject I will return to many times, with its infinite possibilities of mood.'

Breakers
watercolour (7 x 15in)

'The movement of the sea with breaking waves is a constant challenge, whether in storm conditions on Chesil Bank or, as here, in much gentler vein.'

The Pinnacles
watercolour (9 x 11in)

'I was very grateful for the unexpected calm that descended after we had left Swanage on this outing. It enabled me to do some rapid sketching along this stunning stretch of Jurassic Coast. The painting was produced in the studio from the drawings, but with the aid of our photographs to confirm some angles.'

Homeward Bound
acrylic (13 x 24in)

'The stack of Old Harry is clearly seen from North Haven Point on the Sandbanks Peninsula. The harbour mouth always offers me marine material, with plenty from which to pick and choose. It is not usually this quiet.'

Home-turf – Weymouth
∽ and Portland ∾

Weymouth has changed considerably in the artist's lifetime and one of the major improvements has been the Royal Society for the Protection of Birds' stewardship of Radipole Lake, close to the heart of the town. Edward and Geraldine spent happy hours here together in their youth, rowing on the lake and attempting tennis on the nearby municipal courts. Today, the old 'Backwater' is maintained for the benefit of the birds and visitors alike.

There have been other changes. The inner harbour's marina boasts hundreds of yachts and motor cruisers, while the 'tomato boats' no longer ply their trade from the Channel Islands. The old brewery is now home to a museum, a shopping centre and bijou residences and the 'boat train' has not run along the quay for years.

Yet the harbour retains its charm. Holidaymakers can still fish from a boat in the bay or take a trip around Portland Harbour. They will no longer see the Royal Naval vessels or helicopters, as the Navy finally deserted Portland in 1999. Weymouth's crowning glory is its bay, with its girdle of limestone hills to the east which, fortunately, have been altered only by nature's hand.

To the west lies the 'Isle' of Portland, which, like Purbeck, has limestone at the heart of its history. The Causeway connects it to the mainland, as does the mighty, pebbled Chesil Bank. Edward has carried rods and a lamp up over the beach for a night's fishing on many occasions, but not for some years.

His choice of home and working base would have received approval from the Dorset poet and novelist, Thomas Hardy, who wrote the following lines in his Preface to *The Well Beloved* in August, 1912:

To those who know the rocky coign of England here depicted – overlooking the great Channel Highway with all its suggestiveness, and standing out so far into mid-sea that touches of the Gulf Stream soften the air till February – it is matter of surprise that the place has not been more frequently chosen as the retreat of artists and poets in search of inspiration – for at least a month or two in the year, the tempestuous rather than the fine seasons by preference.

For seventeen years, Edward has been nourished by what the island offers. A stroll to view the sea and its canopy of sky is part of his daily routine. Here, the difference in the changing seasons becomes abundantly clear. The skies in his works are often those he has fixed in his mind's eye on these walks, or captured on the easel from his studio window, as a painting is in progress. Artistic licence is a useful tool!

Sanctuary, Radipole
acrylic (13 x 15in)

'I need no excuse to paint the reserve. The willows turn unbelievably bright in autumn and winter and make irresistible subject matter.'

Weymouth Beach
acrylic (13 x 18in)

'The Esplanade and the beach haven't changed much since my youth, but the bulk of the Pier Bandstand was demolished long ago. I remember clearly the potted palms on the stage, the summer beauty contests, the roller-skating sessions and, on one occasion, an evening with Geraldine at the wrestling!'

92

The Nothe, Weymouth
acrylic (9 x 12in)

'The Fort at the entrance to the harbour was completed in 1872 by Royal Engineers and convicts from Portland, but its guns were never fired in anger. Very much part of my childhood daily life, I remember its barbed wire and 'Keep Out' signs. Now it has been renovated and is open to the public.'

Radipole Lake, Weymouth
acrylic (17 x 23in)

'Hiring a rowing boat and taking it down the lake is now a thing of the past, as it is now part of the RSPB reserve. I still have fond memories, some involving mosquito bites and blisters!'

94

Sunlit Reeds, Radipole
acrylic (18 x 14in)

'Weymouth's residents are so lucky to have this oasis close to their town centre – the sedge and reed warblers think so too.'

95

To Portland
acrylic (13 x 18in)

'My framer lived in Abbotsbury for many years and I regularly detoured up Abbotsbury Hill when visiting him, just to take in this view. Many people know it as "the hill with the ice-cream van in the lay-by".'

Summer Holiday
gouache (8 x 10in)

'I expect boys have fished around Ferrybridge on the Portland Causeway for centuries. Plaice and flounder were an easy catch when I was a schoolboy, but are now much rarer.'

Blue Moon
acrylic (13 x 15in)

'A flight of fancy at the easel – I have stood out at Portland Bill in the moonlight, but never with a paintbrush or sketchbook.'

Priory Corner, Portland
acrylic (13 x 18in)

'New Road may have changed its route up the hill, but the stone seat nearby remains on its initial site. It's certainly quieter now the Naval helicopters are no longer based on the harbourside below.'

Coastal Path, Portland
acrylic (7 x 14in)

'I don't know how much longer it will be before this part of the East Cliff tumbles to the sea, but this is a major coastal footpath, so a solution must be found. Meanwhile, the path is still open and we enjoy it while we can.'

The Race
acrylic (13 x 18in)

'What can I say about the sea? It features in most days of my life and I would miss it if I had to live inland.'

Red Crane, Portland Bill
acrylic (17 x 23in)

'Those who visit the Bill, perhaps on a blustery Sunday after lunch, know why it is described as "rugged". By the way, the crane is still used for lower-ing boats to the sea.'

The Light, Portland
acrylic (17 x 23in)

'As a child, I thought the term "Bill" referred to the lighthouse. Of course, the name probably refers to the shape of the tip of the island, like a bird's beak. It must be one of the most well-known lighthouses in the country.'

Out to Pasture
acrylic (7 x 10in)

'Horses, some of them rescued animals, are a feature of island life. These are a few minutes' walk from our home. The daisies spring up out of nowhere every year and disappear almost as fast. The painting belongs to Geraldine.'

Smilers
acrylic (14 x 12in)

'Daisies always find their way into my exhibitions. These were painted in my garden, where weedkiller is not allowed; I leave some groups undisturbed, mowing round them.'

105

STATION, WEST BAY - EV

❧ Quiet Corners ❧

Edward's approach to portraying Dorset's natural glories is to attempt to capture the spirit of the spectacular while elevating the seemingly commonplace to an equal position of rivalry.

This quote is very apt. It is taken from an invitation to the Private View of a past exhibition at Peter Hedley's gallery in Wareham.

His eye can settle on a subject that others may glance at fleetingly, or miss altogether. It is often not the well-known Dorset that catches his eye, but the hidden corners.

Fiddleford Winter
acrylic (13 x 15in)

'The light, overnight snowfall in North Dorset was an unexpected bonus on the day we had set aside to visit the Mill. The last few miles of the car journey from home to Sturminster were very slow, but the footpath walk from there to the Mill was magical.'

Pond, Bulbarrow
acrylic (8 x 15in)

'The Dorset Ridgeway has some excellent vantage points for long-distance views, but the National Trust land at Bulbarrow on the Ridge also has some very gentle subject matter. This was sketched during a lunch stop on a family walk.'

Lane near Frampton
acrylic (13 x 15in)

'Not far from Frampton's busy road is some of the loveliest countryside in the county, with access on a network of footpaths, where time seems to have stood still.'

Stour in Flood
acrylic (16 x 19in)

'When the Stour breaks its banks near Blandford, these meadows drain very slowly. We are told to expect wetter autumns and winters, so I should have plenty of opportunities for this type of subject.'

Stile to Sheep Down
acrylic (14 x 12in)

'In a dip on the road north from Hardy's Monument, this short track leads to Sheep Down, which sweeps to The Winterbournes across ancient field systems and tumuli.'

111

Walking the Dog
acrylic (9 x 11in)

'Dog-walkers are often the only people who pass when I'm sketching and some are naturally curious. I remember the shadows lengthened considerably on this occasion during our chat.'

Eggardon Ox-eyes
acrylic (12 x 15in)

'No apologies for more daisies – they can brighten up any corner and I still enjoy painting them more than any other subject.'

113

Evening, Shillingstone
acrylic (9 x 11in)

'The fading rays of the sun on the cows attracted my interest and I noted down just a few rough shapes. Friesians are a gift in these circumstances as they are easy to see in poor light conditions.'

Coombe Wood, Wool
acrylic (13 x 15in)

'Bluebell is one of the species under threat from climate change, so I now make a point of visiting bluebell woods each spring. Coombe is a small wood at New Buildings, near Wool.'

Little Haven, Mudeford
acrylic (10 x 20in)

'Little Haven is delightful from every angle and, against my usual inclination to avoid buildings in finished works, I have painted them more than once. Hengistbury, in the distance, is another of Dorset's National Trust properties.'

Sunday Sail, Mudeford
oil (10 x 11in)

'Although I have included this painting in the chapter entitled 'Quiet Corners', summer weekends at Mudeford can be anything but quiet, with vessels queuing to return to harbour in early evening. This mid-week day was more to my liking and it was the striped sail that stopped me initially.'

The Stour at Sturminster
acrylic   (8 x 10in)

'Thomas Hardy lived with his wife on the hillside only a few yards from this bend in the river and they were reportedly very happy at Sturminster.'

Summer
acrylic (12 x 9in)

'What would summer be without poppies on the kerbsides and at the edges of meadows? We found these in an overgrown, deserted orchard.'

Harvest
acrylic (17 x 23in)

'At Muckleford, near Dorchester, these haybales looked like they had been carelessly tossed down the hill. The composition of the fields and hills was just asking to be used. I can't describe how different a day sketching in the countryside feels from one on the coast, but the whole process can seem to be more leisurely.'

Sunshine and Shadows
acrylic (10 x 11in)

'Near the Dorset Ridgeway, again on National Trust land. I used intensely dark and light tones, aiming to convey a feeling of heat and shade.'

Trees at Bulbarrow
acrylic (10 x 11in)

'This group of hawthorns and ash had such personality that it warranted a work to itself, rather than being incidental in a larger landscape.'

Near Spetisbury
acrylic (9 x 11in)

'Past this spot, up the winding road, is Spetisbury. Their superb bridge all but vanishes under the Frome in flood but, luckily, the village is on higher ground.'

West along the Fleet
acrylic (10 x 20in)

'The famous Abbotsbury Swannery is tucked behind the trees in the middle distance. The Chesil Bank has so many visitors that a wooden walkway has been positioned up and over the bank at this spot. This is easier on the feet, but also protects the beach.'

Edge of the Field
acrylic (9 x 11in)

'I confess to not knowing exactly where this is, but my sketchbook places it in North Dorset. I sometimes note the locations in the book, but often rely on memory. My working methods may have to change as time goes by!'

Riverbank
acrylic (11 x 10in)

'The main Dorchester to Yeovil road passes behind the trees at this idyllic spot by Muckleford's hump-back bridge. We've watched yellow wagtails and kingfishers here and the bridge is ideal for "Pooh-sticks", as long as you watch for traffic.'

To Maiden Castle
acrylic (8 x 10in)

'I will occasionally take a broader approach to landscape, with bolder, freer brushstrokes and this is the result. This sign-posted footpath is off the Dorchester to Martinstown road.'

Pastoral
acrylic (7 x 14in)

'West of Dorchester, near Frampton, this circular walk on public paths takes in ancient woodland, a valley bottom and formal parkland. It can be completed in a couple of hours or, with a sketchbook and paints, in around seven!'

Fordington, Dorchester
acrylic (13 x 15in)

'Dorchester is blessed with these water-meadows around its north-eastern boundaries, easily accessed near Grey's Bridge or at Hangman's Cottage. It's a pleasant, level footpath walk from here all the way to Charminster.'

129

Hambledon Hill
acrylic (13 x 15in)

'The grandeur of this hill fort is clear from the tiny hamlet of Hammoon. The name sounds like it belongs to the Highlands of Scotland, but it is, of course, in North Dorset.'

Lydlinch Common
watercolour (10 x 7in)

'Alongside the Sturminster to Sherborne road, Lydlinch Common in late summer is an undisturbed haven of colour and texture, perfectly suited to this watercolour technique.'

TREELINE - EV

~ 'Max Gate', Dorchester ~

After we opened the house to the public, one of the early requests was for an image of 'Max Gate'. We did not have to search for too long for a local artist who might produce what we wanted, as the Peter Hedley Gallery instantly recommended one of their best-selling artists.

Upon meeting Edward, we were immediately struck by both the man and his paintings – the perfect artist to become associated with the life, work and home of Dorset's most famous literary figure, Thomas Hardy. He soon became our Artist-in-Residence. Edward is Dorset born and bred and his detailed work is centred on the beauty and colours of his beloved county in all weathers and all seasons. Now his skies billow over Hardy's lush countryside and dramatic coastline in the wealth of work on permanent exhibition at 'Max Gate'.

It was not difficult to match a quote from Thomas Hardy with every painting on display at the house, some of which are included amongst those on the following pages. Hardy's work notes every change of the landscape in its varied moods and we are certain he would have appreciated Edward's attention to such details.

We were told initially that 'this artist does not do prints'. For us, and for Hardy, he readily made an exception. Peter's recommendation hit the target: the painting of 'Max Gate' is popular with our visitors from around the world, our walls are adorned with gems and, most importantly, we can count Edward and Geraldine as our friends.

ANDREW AND MARILYN LEAH
National Trust tenants of 'Max Gate', Dorchester

'*Max Gate*'
acrylic (9 x 10in)

'Thomas Hardy lived at "Max Gate" from 1885 to 1928. The painting was commissioned and is available as a print at the house.'

Egdon
acrylic (6 x 8in)

Overhead the hollow stretch of whitish cloud shutting out the sky was as a tent which had the whole heath for its floor. The heaven being spread with this pallid screen and the earth with the darkest vegetation, their meeting line at the horizon was clearly marked.
The Return of the Native

The Frome, Bockhampton
acrylic (11 x 10in)

*The Froom waters were clear as the pure
River of Life…*
                    Tess of the d'Urbervilles

Maiden Castle, East
acrylic (11 x 15in)

With the shifting of the clouds the faces of the steeps vary in colour and in shade, broad lights appearing where mist and vagueness had prevailed, dissolving in their turn into melancholy gray, which spreads over and eclipses the luminous bluffs. In this so-thought immutable spectacle all is change.

A Tryst at an Ancient Earthwork

Cottage Garden
gouache (10 x 7in)

Red Roses, lilacs, variegated box Are there in plenty,
and such hardy flowers As flourish best untrained.
                                                    'Domicilium'

137

Ten Hatches
acrylic (11 x 15in)

The river here was deep and strong at all times, and the hatches on this account were raised and lowered by cogs and a winch.
The Mayor of Casterbridge

138

Bournemouth Beach
acrylic (13 x 18in)

This fashionable watering place…; a Mediterranean lounging place on the English Channel.
Tess of the d'Urbervilles

Path, Thorncombe
acrylic (9 x 11in)

Heart-halt and spirit-lame, City-opprest, Unto this wood I came As to a nest;
'In a Wood'

West to Lulworth
acrylic (13 x 18in)

He descended and came to a small basin of sea enclosed by the cliffs. Troy's nature freshened within him; he thought he would rest and bathe here before going further.
Far from the Madding Crowd

South from Hartland
acrylic (11 x 15in)

…crossed the bridge over the moat and rode under the first archway into the outer ward.   The Hand of Ethelberta (Corfe Castle is Hardy's *Corvsgate*)

Old Harry Rocks
acrylic (17 x 23in)

...a corner called Old Harry Point, which lay about halfway along their track, and stood, with its detached posts and stumps of white rock, like a skeleton's lower jaw, grinning at British Navigation.
The Hand of Ethelberta

⁓ Further Reading ⁓

Philip Jamison *Capturing Nature in Watercolour* (Watson-Guptill Publications, 1980)

Norman Battershill *Painting Landscapes in Oil* (BT Batsford Ltd, 1997)

Norman Battershill *Light on the Landscape* (Pitman, London, 1977)

David Curtis *A Light Touch* (David & Charles, 1994)

Ferdinand Petrie *Drawing Landscapes in Pencil* (Watson-Guptill Publications, 1979)

Helen A Cooper *Winslow Homer Watercolours* (Yale University Press, 1986)

Denys Brook-Hart *20th Century British Marine Paintings* (Antique Collectors Club Ltd, 1981)

Adrian Hill *Sketching and Painting Out of Doors* (Blandford Press, 1961)

Barry Miles *Edward Wesson 1910–1983* (Halsgrove, 1999)

John Blockley *The Challenge of Watercolour* (Adam & Charles Black, 1979)

Trevor Chamberlain *Light and Atmosphere in Watercolour* (David & Charles, 1999)

John Miller *Leave Tomorrow Behind* (The Studio Fine Art Publications, 1989)

Percy V Bradshaw & Ernest W Hazlehust *I Wish I Could Paint* (The Studio Publications, London & New York, 1945)

Edward Seago A *Canvas to Cover* (Collins, London, 1947)

Rowland Hilder *Sketching Country* (The Herbert Press, London, 1991)

Jack Merriott *Discovering Watercolour* (Pitman, London, 1973)